PARIS IN PHOTOGRAPHS 1890s

INTRODUCTION AND CAPTIONS BY
Alex Toledano

CALLA EDITIONS
MINEOLA, NEW YORK

Bibliographical Note

Paris in Photographs, 1890s, is a new work, first published by Calla Editions in 2015.

International Standard Book Number

ISBN-13: 978-1-60660-051-1
ISBN-10: 1-60660-051-6

Calla Editions
An Imprint of Dover Publications, Inc.
www.callaeditions.com

Printed in China by C & C Joint Printing CO., (GUANGDONG) LTD.

Introduction

*T*his album's first photograph, depicting the Galerie d'Apollon inside the Louvre, is magical. The room, designed by Louis XIV's team of architects, decorators, and artists, glistens in the glowing light. The sculptural reliefs along the left wall and ceiling, stripped by the camera of their gilding and extravagant colors, escape a two-dimensional destiny and seem to be chiseled out by the interplay of light and shadow. All of the furniture and exposed objects rest neatly in their linear layout without a soul in sight to disturb them. The photographer has made this monumental Baroque hall, which was designed to overwhelm the senses with color, luxury, and excess, into a refined, atmospheric stillness that calms more than it excites.

Although the places and scenes in this album's fifty images vary—from interior to exterior, from scenes of daily life to perfectly framed monuments—the photos all bring a similar order and tranquility to the city that they represent. Flip through these images as an American in the 1890s may have, and you will see a grand, elegant yet fresh Paris, filled with some of the world's great architectural monuments, modern boulevards, and a thriving commercial center that is vibrant but not too busy.

This representation of Paris should not be surprising to anyone—the city is depicted at its best in these photos taken in the late 1880s and early 1890s, in the manner that continues to be used to attract more visitors than any other city in the world. This album was sold primarily to tourists and visitors who wanted to cherish their memories. Now, over 120 years later, this way of photographing Paris has become the standard, iconic way of depicting the city—a postcard view of Paris.

The publishers and likely photographers of the album, the Neurdein Brothers (known in French as Neurdein Frères), were masters of the genre.[1] They sold photo albums of high-quality albumen silver prints showing popular destinations in France and North Africa. The Neurdein Brothers represented each location in a manner that they imagined would sell well. Symmetry, dramatic shadow and light, impressive views from above, and simple compositions were hallmarks of their style, all designed to showcase their photographs' subjects as vividly as possible. They would carry their heavy, large-format cameras and seek out the best possible times of day and vantage points to photograph a monument, landmark, or scene. Since preparing each photo and then developing the glass plates in a mobile darkroom on site was an elaborate and expensive process, they would try to make each shot as well

---

[1] For the factual information on the Neurdein Frères that follows, see John Hannavy, ed. *Encyclopedia of Nineteenth-Century Photography,* Vol. 2. New York: Routledge, 2008. 991–992.

thought-out as possible. Their photographs were the antithesis of snapshots—they were premeditated, composed, and designed to depict their subjects in the best possible manner. In 1898, their way of representing landmarks became even more dominant when they were given control of managing and adding to the French government's archives of photographs of historical monuments.

Over the course of the 1890s and into the first decade of the twentieth century, as the Neurdein Brothers' business grew, they purchased new printing machinery that allowed them to take advantage of the growing business in postcards. The same photographs that they had used in this photo album, for example, were later cheaply printed as postcards and would be reproduced in quantities previously unthinkable. As one of the largest postcard producers in France—which, as a nation, was printing approximately 300 million postcards per year by 1907—their images and method of depicting monuments were widely circulated and viewed.[2] Their images became the iconic postcard pictures of Paris.

These are photographs of privilege. Even when the photos are of the everyday and do not hide the bustle of Paris's streets (see Plates 7 and 19, for example), the viewer sees the city from above, looking out over its activity, avoiding the congestion, noise, and energy. In this album there is not a single photograph of street life taken from the ground from the perspective of a pedestrian. For all of the street shots, the camera is perched either at the top of a ladder or from the window of a building. The Neurdein Brothers did this for practical reasons, as it produced more expansive, panoramic images without too many heads getting in the way of the landscape. But in the process, the pictures were lifted above the fray, transporting the viewer above the density of people and activity on the ground and providing a special way of seeing the city.

Paris was a city worth seeing in this manner at the time. Beyond its older monuments—the Louvre, the Tuileries Gardens, Notre Dâme, Sainte-Chapelle—a new Paris was all the rage for visitors. The city had been drastically transforming its image since the 1850s and had a new look, one that no other city in the world could boast. Even the older monuments looked fresh, as urban planners had demolished many of their surrounding buildings to liberate them from the dense urban landscape around them and to allow them to be seen from a distance and captured as a whole by the lens of the camera.

As the standard, slightly-oversimplified story goes, after Louis Napoleon, the nephew of Napoleon, anointed himself Napoleon III, Emperor of France, in 1852, he chose to rethink and refashion Paris, with the help of his local administrator, Georges-Eugène Haussmann, the Prefect of Paris. Using dictatorial powers, Napoleon III and Haussmann demolished approximately forty percent of the city's buildings in order to create wide boulevards, grand apartment buildings, public parks, and fresh monuments fit not only for an emperor but for the growing middle classes. In the decades that followed,

[2] Leonard Pitt, *Paris Postcards: The Golden Age*. Berkeley, CA: Counterpoint, 2009. xix.

leading up until World War I, these areas were gradually redeveloped, creating the city we know so well today. Paris became the first historic city made modern in one fell swoop and it was this newly reinvented city—a mix of past and present—that attracted the world to its doorstep.

In this album of albumen prints found on the dusty shelves of the Dover archives, we see fifty images of Paris and its surrounding area, many of which seem so iconic and perfect that there does not seem to be much to say about them. What is surprising about these images is what is left out of them. Paris and France were surprisingly imperfect at the time. The city, behind this glamorous new façade, was undergoing significant, sometimes messy, changes that turned it into a battleground of different ideas, people, and ways of life. Paris in the 1890s was the opposite of neat and orderly, despite many wishing it were and the proliferation of images that show it as such.

*T*raditional historical narratives describe the end of the nineteenth-century in France as the Belle Époque. At first glance, this period left us with great cultural artifacts: the beginnings of modern art, the rise of mass popular culture, the World's Fairs (*Expositions Universelles*) that drew tens of millions of visitors to Paris in 1878, 1889, and 1900, and some of the greatest examples of architecture and engineering, including the Eiffel Tower, the Grand and Petit Palais, as well as the underground metro system and the rise of automobiles. This vision of the late-nineteenth century as an important cultural and technological turning point in Paris is not incorrect. But to privilege these stories and to view the end of the century and the beginning of the twentieth as a gradual path to prosperity that eventually explodes into World War I in 1914, would be to neglect important events and currents in French history.

To start, politics in late-nineteenth century Paris were especially volatile. The Third Republic, France's eighteen-year-old fragile democracy, had been on the verge of being dismantled by what would have been a publicly supported coup led by General Georges Boulanger in 1889. Parisians had elected him as their deputy and he could have quickly consolidated his supporters to let him take power over the nation. Instead, he acted slowly, and his opponents pounced on him and tried to arrest him for treason. He soon fled the country and the Republic continued cautiously into its next decade.

Soon after, a new case of treason against the French military captain, Alfred Dreyfus, consumed the nation, only to be exposed in 1898 as an anti-Semitic setup. As the trial during the Dreyfus Affair was ongoing in 1899, a coup was attempted by the far right during the funeral of the Republican president, Félix Faure. Terrorism was common throughout the decade and worker strikes became more frequent with May Day becoming a national day of protest for the first time in 1898. Abroad, the French army had entered into its most aggressive phase of imperialism, fighting difficult wars all over the Asian and African continents, which often had negative effects in the metropole. The decade between Boulanger and Dreyfus was, according to Susanna Barrows, a historian of nineteenth-century France, a moment "which only a café devotee or a casual tourist would call 'gay.'"[3]

The newspapers and periodicals of the era obsessively covered all of these events, among many others, with zeal. Just as this was the great era of the mass-produced postcard, it was also one of the most successful periods for tabloids and the press in general. These affordable publications were filled with stories of scandal, crime, and immorality, contributing to a general feeling of a society in decay.[4] *Fin de siècle* was an overused, general adjective, which described an immoral, anxiety-inducing, negative period in time. As Eugen Weber, a historian of France, writes, "an 1888 play called *Fin de Siècle* turns around shady deals, adultery, and murder; a dreary novel of the same title, published in 1889, tells of a rich young man [for] whom boredom, gambling, and misplaced affections lead to suicide in 325 weary pages."[5] The moment was not optimistic and Parisians were fearful of their future.

The link between postcard images and a popular press is not tangential. Both were ways to sell cheaply printed material to a public hungry to communicate, read, and consume. While the customers were different, the mass media's need to sell always catered to the imaginary—to the desires of tourists who bought postcards and the fears of locals who bought newspapers. Both views of Paris—one calm, elegant, and beautiful; the other frightening, degenerating, and filthy—are products of the rise of a new literate and international middle class, eager to see new places, break down social boundaries, and use its new wealth and education to make itself more aware of its home as well as the world around it. The Neurdein Brothers' photo album offers one of those views of Paris, meaningful not only for the city it presents but the one it avoided.

ALEX TOLEDANO

---

[3] Susanna Barrows, *Distorted Mirrors: Visions of the Crowd in Late Nineteenth-Century France.* New Haven, CT: Yale University Press, 1981. 2. See the book's introduction for an elegant, concise introduction to French political and social upheaval at the end of the nineteenth century.

[4] See Eugen Weber, *France, Fin de Siècle.* Cambridge, MA: Belknap Press, 1986 for a thorough study of this fear of erosion throughout French society.

[5] Weber, 1986. 10.

ABOUT THE AUTHOR

Alex Toledano received his PhD in Late Modern European History at the University of California, Berkeley, and specializes in the history of Paris neighborhoods since the French Revolution. His dissertation, *Sharing Paris: The Use and Ownership of a Neighborhood, Its Streets, and Public Spaces, 1950–2012*, studies the roles of visitors and residents in shaping community and daily life in Parisian neighborhoods. Based in Paris, he is the co-founder and President of VISTO Images, an art consulting firm that curates art programs for luxury properties and private collections around the world.

PLATES

Musée du Louvre, la Galerie d'Apollon

A black-and-white representation of a room that explodes in front of your eyes in gilded flamboyance can never quite tell the story properly. The Galerie d'Apollon of the Louvre, though, as it is depicted here, somehow reveals itself despite our color blindness. The luxurious textures and intricate interplay of the fabrics, bas-relief, sculpture, and painting shine through in the glowing light. The decorative extravagance sought out by Louis XIV appears softened here by the lens of the camera, bringing calm to a hyperactive space.

PLATE 1

Palais du Louvre, la Colonnade

The easternmost façade of the Louvre was the result of a seventeenth-century architectural competition in which Claude Perrault beat out Gian Lorenzo Bernini to design Louis XIV's new wing of the Louvre (note the "LL" sculpted seals on the left). Known as Perrault's Colonnade, this classical architectural masterpiece departs from the contemporary Baroque design inside the Louvre seen in the previous photograph (Plate 1). It looks even more pristine and composed in this image than it does today. The well-manicured garden and its sculpture have since disappeared, the green replaced by the building's excavated medieval moat and pebble-strewn dirt.

PLATE 2

Perspective des Sept Ponts

In order to get this view of old Paris, the Seine, and the city's newest addition, the Eiffel Tower (built in 1889 for the World's Fair), the photographer climbed to the very top of the Église Saint-Gervais-et-Saint-Protais on the Right Bank. We see the Arc de Triomphe in the far distance on the right, and in the close foreground on the right, the back of the church's façade. Behind it, lies the Hôtel de Ville, Paris's city hall that had recently been rebuilt after having been destroyed during the fighting between the city's forces and the French army during the Paris Commune in 1871. Just to its left, in between two rows of planted trees, lies a sculpture of a man, Étienne Marcel, on a horse, facing the Île de la Cité. In the fourteenth century he led a successful rebellion of Parisians against the French king. Staring out toward the island, the historic center of the church and state's power, the sculpture lets both parties know that Paris will never lose its independence.

La Rive Gauche de la Cité

Taken from the same location as the previous picture (Plate 3), the photographer has turned to the left, now looking south toward Notre Dâme on the Île de la Cité and, beyond it, toward the Left Bank and its neoclassical Panthéon on the left. It is the stillness and emptiness of the Seine—except for the back of a boat on the left—that is so surprising. Before cars, trucks, and highways, and with the railroad system still in its infancy, the Seine was Paris's main shipping artery. The river here seems more like a swimming pool than a commercial passageway.

Vue prise en Amont du Ponte Royal

As in the previous picture (Plate 4), the main monuments depicted are Notre Dâme in the center and the Panthéon on the far right in the distance. Looking southeast from the top of a tower in the Louvre, the photographer does not hide the industrial activity along the Seine. We see a number of boats and barges as well as deposits of sand and stone that they have left along the banks, imported to fuel the city's construction boom. We also see the Pont des Arts, now famous as a pedestrian bridge, shown with a blur of traffic crossing the river.

PLATE 5

11

Le Nouveau Louvre

The photographer has remained inside the Louvre but has taken this photo from the opposite side of the same building, looking out onto the courtyard. Today's pyramid was then a landscaped garden with a monument to Léon Gambetta, one of the founders of the French Third Republic in the 1870s, at its center. This is a rare image in the album where contemporary politics are visible. The long exposure of the photograph makes the square feel empty except for a few people who remained still—all of the horses and wagons are gray, almost invisible blurs along the roadway.

PLATE 6

L'Avenue de l'Opéra

Here, looking northwest, we see the pure magnificence of Haussmann's renovation of Paris, the Boulevard de l'Opéra, which he blazed through the older streets of the First Arrondissement. His idea was simple, pure, and elegant—to link Napoleon III's new Opéra, pictured at the center at the end of the boulevard, to the Louvre, lining the road with the most fashionable modern buildings. The plan never fully materialized, as the government never received permission to demolish the last building that separated the Louvre from the boulevard, now the Hôtel du Louvre (not associated with the museum). The photographer took his photo from the window of this building.

Le Jardin du Palais Royal

The privileged grounds behind the seventeenth-century Palais Royal are depicted as perfectly as possible here, the fountain appearing as a sculpture of water, the grounds empty of the life that filled them. The arcades on the ground floor of the buildings surrounding the garden catered to all classes and were known to contain some of the most fashionable cafés and restaurants in the city as well as working-class haunts. Prostitutes were also known to solicit work along the sidelines of the gardens.

PLATE 8

La Place Vendôme

We get a glimpse here into the daily life of the ritzy neighborhoods of Paris in this view onto the Place Vendôme and its column commemorating Napoleon's victory in Austerlitz. Horse-drawn carriages—some seeking customers, others full—lead people to shops like the furrier on the left corner. Many well-dressed pedestrians also traverse the streets. In order to get this view from above, it seems that the photographer took this picture from the top of a ladder.

La Rue de Rivoli & le Jardin des Tuileries

The Rue de Rivoli is cleverly depicted here as the reflection of the Tuileries Garden. The street, despite its traffic, seems still and impeccably neat. The potted trees in the Tuileries—which no longer exist and have been replaced with an amusement park in the summer—almost resemble the staggered coaches on the street as they recede into the distance.

La Place de la Concorde

Once the site of the frequently-used guillotine during the French Revolution, the Place de la Concorde as it is seen here had been significantly transformed once it became a more peaceful location in the city. One of the most recent architectural additions to the Place de la Concorde in this photo is, surprisingly, the ancient Egyptian obelisk, erected in 1836, soon after it had been given by the Ottoman Viceroy in Egypt to the French king, Louis Philippe. Accompanying the addition of the obelisk was a redesign of the square and its fountains, including the addition of female sculptures representing the major French cities in its corners (two are visible, almost white, in the far left and right corners). Strasbourg (not included in the picture), however, was covered in a black cloth as it had been lost to the Germans in the Franco-Prussian War of 1870. After World War I, when the French regained sovereignty over Strasbourg, the statue was unveiled.

La Grande Allée du Jardin des Tuileries

The long exposure has rendered pristine this view of the Le Nôtre-designed Tuileries Garden that looks out onto the Place de la Concorde and the Arc de Triomphe in the distance, the *grande axe* of Paris. We are left with a serene scene of three people strolling to the right of the pond, enjoying their leisure time, and a girl in a white dress in the foreground on the right. Erased in a painterly blur is all the activity in front of the girl and the other people moving in the park, who have disappeared thanks to the tricks of the camera lens.

L'Arc de Triomphe

The Arc de Triomphe stands triumphantly in this three-quarter view taken from a nearby building that accentuates the arch but shows the monument's mass and depth. It appears even more monumental in this image than in person, dwarfing the city—both its buildings and people—that surround it. It is a rare image in the album in which Paris no longer feels like a city built to human scale.

L'Avenue des Champs-Élysées

The Champs Élysées extends here from the Place de la Concorde toward the Arc de Triomphe. This short exposure does not hide the activity on the street and allows us to see people using transportation up close. Rather than seeing automobiles that conceal their passengers, we can observe the people here, like the two men sitting next to each other on the carriage in the front center, engrossed in conversation as they drive along.

Le Palais du Trocadéro

The Trocadéro Palace, completed in 1878 for the World's Fair and situated across the river from the Eiffel Tower after it was built in 1889 (see Plate 18), is depicted as majestically as possible in this picture, with its fountains and garden enhancing the symmetry of its neo-Byzantine, Orientalist design. After the fair, the building was transformed from its first use as a massive exhibition hall with a concert hall twice the size of the Opéra Garnier into the home of a variety of smaller institutions. These included France's first ethnographic museum, the Museum of French Monuments, as well as the Indochinese Museum and an observatory. The Trocadéro Palace was considered too old-fashioned and dated by many critics and was eventually destroyed in the 1930s in favor of the more modern and minimalist Palais de Chaillot that currently stands in its place.

L'Avenue des Champs-Élysées

Here we view the Champs Élysées from the opposite side as in Plate 14, now looking down upon it from the top of the Arc de Triomphe. Very few pedestrians walk down the sidewalks and most of the activity on the street is of carriages passing through the center traffic lanes. We see Notre Dâme in the distance just to the right of the center and the Panthéon on the right, as well as the Palais d'Industrie, the large glass structure just after the right wing of the Champs Élysées ends. This structure, built in the style of London's Crystal Palace, was later knocked down in 1897 to make way for the Grand Palais, one of the architectural stars of the 1900 World's Fair.

L'Hôtel des Invalides

The Église du Dôme was a late addition to the complex known as Les Invalides, built under the order of Louis XIV as a military hospital and rehabilitation center for veterans of the French army. Louis XIV hired the famous architect, Jules Hardouin-Mansart, to design a Baroque royal chapel on the site. The photographer accentuates the façade's symmetry by precisely framing the building, including even the lampposts in the very foreground to balance the image. At the time of the photograph, Napoleon's body was entombed inside the chapel, and Alfred Dreyfus had recently had his military rank stripped from him in front of the church due to a fabricated anti-Semitic charge of treason.

PLATE 17

Paris

La Tour Eiffel

This picture, taken during the 1889 World's Fair, the *Exposition Universelle*, captures the stands and tents erected to receive the more than 30 million visitors who came to Paris to see the latest advances in technology, engineering, and manufacturing, as well as examples of many traditional cultures from around the world, often represented in demeaning, controversial ways. For the duration of the fair, Paris was an amusement park and this was the center of it. After the exhibition had finished, all of the buildings and structures were knocked down on the Champs de Mars except for the newly built Eiffel Tower. The surrounding streets soon became filled with the most expensive, fashionable buildings in the French capital, thanks to the raging success—despite the initial controversy—of the iron tower.

Paris

PLATE 18

L'Opéra, Académie Nationale de Musique

The photographer has approached the Opéra built by Charles Garnier to show it up close (see Plate 7 for the view from a distance). As the most important and expensive Parisian monument constructed during the reign of Napoleon III (though the building only opened in 1875, five years after he abdicated), the Opéra soon became the cultural center of the Parisian elite. Shown here during the daytime, we see that despite its grandeur, the city around it was bustling and erratic. Here we see a two-horse-drawn, double-decker omnibus, which at the time was the main form of public transportation, in this instance bringing passengers from Madeleine to Bastille.

Le Grand-Escalier de l'Opéra

The Grand Escalier of the Opéra is shown here much as the Galerie d'Apollon in the Louvre (see Plate 1)—bathed in dramatic light that brings the space to life. This extravagant, impressive centerpiece to the public areas of the building was meant to dazzle the eyes with its variety of materials—many different colored types of marble, onyx, copper, mirrors, glass, plaster, stucco, etc.—that jump out even in this black-and-white, two-dimensional photograph.

PLATE 20

Paris

La Porte Saint-Martin

The tone of the album changes here with this photo that depicts Louis XIV's two triumphal arches, the Porte Saint-Martin and the Porte Saint-Denis (in the distance), each built in the 1670s to serve the dual purpose of commemorating the king's military victories and marking the entrance to Paris from its northern suburbs. Here, the teeming life of the working-class neighborhoods along the Grands Boulevards has become the subject of the photo more than the monuments themselves. On the left, we see horse-drawn taxi drivers sporting top hats, chatting as they wait for customers. Note the spiral staircase on the outside of the double-decker omnibus, which led passengers to an open-air second level. We also see the written word depicted on buildings, so common at the time, but largely absent from this album. Billboards covered the city's buildings and here they include an advertisement for training in cutting clothing and fabric (the neighborhood was located near the heart of the clothing manufacturing industry) as well as for a place to dance to Polish mazurkas.

PLATE 21

La Place de la Bourse

Finance meets the streets of Paris in this photo depicting the Place de la Bourse and its monumental Palais Brongniart, completed in 1827 to serve as a meeting point for bankers, traders, and financiers. Here they fill its steps and shaded portico as they converse. The neoclassical building was imagined by its creators as a place to facilitate meetings and discussions, which we can consider a success based on the visual evidence of this picture. The neighborhood surrounding the Bourse was one of the most outgoing in Paris—it attracted so many visitors every day that in the 1890s it contained approximately one café per resident. Balzac, however, saw the busy activity as the thief of the square's natural beauty, which to him only came out at night in its emptiness under the "clair de lune."

La Pont au Change & le Palais de Justice

This photo of the newly-reconstructed Pont au Change (see Napoleon III's "N" insignia above the bridge's piers) became a best-selling postcard for the Neurdein Frères. It shows here the orderly passage of foot and wheeled traffic between the Right Bank and the Île de la Cité, whose thirteenth-century palace complex is depicted here (see the Concièrgerie and Sainte-Chapelle, whose roof and spire appear on the left in the distance). Here, one of the greatest medieval monuments left standing in Paris is shown perfectly integrated into the modern activity of the city.

La Tour Saint-Jacques

The Tour Saint-Jacques is a vestige of the city's pre-Revolutionary past. It was built in the early sixteenth-century as part of the church of Saint Jacques-de-la-Boucherie, which, except for the tower, was destroyed in the early years of the Revolution along with many other symbols of the Catholic Church in Paris. It is still unclear why it was spared, but the City of Paris continued to make use of it for more secular affairs. Beginning in 1891, the city created a meteorological platform at its summit above the bell tower.

PLATE 24

Paris

La Cathédrale, Eglise Notre-Dâme

This is a perfect representation of Notre Dâme in all its grandeur after Haussmann opened up the monument by demolishing many of its surrounding buildings. This was part of a grand project to make the city's great monuments more accessible to visitors, more visible, and more photographable. This picture's long exposure erased many of the passers-by letting the monument stand out even more. This perspective would have been impossible to create 40 years earlier, when the Hôtel Dieu, a hospital historically tied to the cathedral, would have blocked this view. The Hôtel Dieu had straddled both sides of the Seine, using the river as its central courtyard, but was moved in the 1860s to the north side of the square, just to the left of the picture's edge, to a more modern building. The vestiges of the old hospital can be seen down the steps to the river where, just behind the man looking out into the water, lies a blocked-off door once used to access the razed hospital. The door still exists today.

PLATE 25

La Nef de l'Eglise Notre-Dâme

The central nave of Notre Dâme, finished in the early fourteenth century and constructed over a period of 160 years, is empty of people but filled with the glow of light above the church's altar. The Neurdein Frères use the same technique to depict this interior as they did for the more modern and extravagant galleries in the Opéra Garnier and the Louvre (Plates 31 and 1, respectively). Even though the colorful light of the stained glass window is missing, its ethereal effect is still captured in this picture.

Plate 26

Tombeau de Napoléon 1er (Hôtel des Invalides)

This is a very different chapel than the one depicted in the previous photograph (Plate 26) and was constructed much more quickly, over a period of twenty years. It was built to hold the relics of a man who was never a saint but who approached that status based on the number of "pilgrims" who came to visit his body after it was returned to France in the 1840s. The bright white stone stands out here, showing Napoleon's resting place as a Baroque-Classical sanctuary within the Invalides. The image links Napoleon and God, with all lines in the composition pointing to the cross above and tomb below.

PLATE 27

Paris

L'Église de la Madeleine

Paris hides in this image, in which the photographer chose to show the Église de la Madeleine as separate and distinct from the city. He was successful except for the few buildings that peek out on both sides behind the church and for the unavoidable fact that the camera must have been standing on a balcony across the square. Empty and enormous, the church is shown as a heavy, imposing Greek temple. The photographer plays with the repetition of form and shadow of the columns, as in many of the interior pictures in this album.

Le Boulevard de la Madeleine

The photographer simply moved his camera to the right from the previous photograph (Plate 28), although it was taken at a different time of year, as the trees no longer have leaves. Here he shows the corner of the Église de la Madeleine and the ultra-fashionable Boulevard de la Madeleine that leads to the Opéra Garnier. We now see that the calmness of the previous picture was a very selective representation of the monument. The stillness and quiet disappear here as we can imagine the noise and energy of the crowds, carriages, omnibuses, and horses that pulled them.

PLATE 29

Boulevard des Capucines, le Grand-Hôtel

The photographer has taken the Boulevard de la Madeleine and its continuation, the Boulevard des Capucines, to the Place de l'Opéra and is looking back down it towards Madeleine (he has also, relative to Plate 19, simply moved forward and pointed the camera to the left). We see the fashionable Café de la Paix on the right, one of the most celebrated addresses for the elite during the Belle Époque, in the context of its noisy surroundings and clogged streets. Its stunning interiors, as well as those of the Opéra (see Plate 31), must have been as much an oasis from the streets as they are now.

PLATE 30

Le Foyer Public de l'Opéra

The photographer again depicts an elegant, extravagant interior, the Grand Foyer of the Opéra Garnier, in perfect light, accentuating the drama and textures of its architecture and furnishings (see Plates 1 and 20). The view out the door on the left into the Great Staircase contributes to the effect of overwhelming opulence, making the space's depth shrink into an ornamented flatness.

PLATE 31

Le Boulevard des Italiens

The photographer has moved east from his position in Plate 30, down to the end of the Boulevard des Italiens near the Rue Drouot, looking back west toward the Madeleine. This is a rare opportunity, as in Plates 7, 16, and 29, for the photographer to have the luxury of depicting a boulevard from high up, as there is a tall building at its end from which it is possible to photograph from the higher floors. On the left in the foreground we see two rows of tables on the street, the early beginnings of the terrace and street dining, where guests wanted to be outside while eating and drinking to participate in the spectacle of the street.

PLATE 32

La Place de la République

Descending closer to street level, the camera has found itself in the middle of the Rue du Temple, looking out onto the Place de la République. The statue of the Republic looks down on the busy spectacle of working-class Paris. We see here in close detail the passengers on an omnibus destined for Vincennes, to the east of Paris, as well as men on the left who are pulling carts, and the numerous kiosks—a new arrival along Paris's sidewalks—selling newspapers and other items. This may be the image in the album that best visualizes the feeling of life on a typical, busy Parisian street in the 1890s.

Le Parc des Battes-Chaumont

Time stands still in this picture of spectators looking out at a massive geological formation. While we see the small gazebo-like structure at its top as well as a house in the distance on the right, the photographers have brought us far from the center of Paris to a place where nature, not man, appears to be shaping the landscape. But in fact, this picture shows one of the most drastic interventions under Haussmann's term, the creation of the Buttes-Chaumont Park in the northeast of Paris in the Nineteenth Arrondissement. This rock formation was created in the 1860s using dynamite and the pond was constructed soon after. The woman on the left reveals the long exposure, turning around to look at the camera and captured in four distinct images as she moved.

Place de la Bastille, la Colonne de Juillet

The Place de la Bastille—where the famous prison of the Revolution once stood—is depicted in the dramatic light just before sunset. Every person and object casts a great shadow eastward, and the column commemorating the Revolution stands as a majestic beacon, shot from the perfect height and angle so that it lies completely above the city. Behind it we see the now demolished Gare de la Bastille, the train station that was replaced in the 1980s by the new home of the French National Opéra, a decision many preservationists still decry.

PLATE 35

Paris

L'Hôtel de Ville

From the Île-de-la-Cité we see the Hôtel de Ville—Paris's city hall—from a different angle than in Plate 3. We can better see the Gothic Revival style in which it was reconstructed in the 1880s following its destruction during the Paris Commune in 1871 at the hands of the French army fighting against the Parisian separatists. Although closed for business, we can see the stands run by the *bouquinistes* along the Seine—here numbered 73 to 77—where booksellers had operated from fixed locations rented by the city since 1859. We also see, on the left, a large barge, the likes of which we no longer see traveling down the Seine.

La Sainte-Chapelle

Sainte-Chapelle, the thirteenth-century jewel of Parisian churches, has a hard time standing out as other monuments do in the photos taken by the Neurdein Frères. As it remains concealed by other buildings in the palace complex on the Île de la Cité, we do not get a full view of it. Its lower level is missing and it seems crowded in by its surroundings. The church was built by Louis IX, also known as Saint Louis, the only French king to achieve sainthood. This private chapel was one of the reasons why he was considered the most pious of French kings. Louis constructed it in less than ten years—incredibly quickly at the time, especially relative to its neighbor, Notre Dâme, which took 160 years to complete—in order to house the Crown of Thorns, which he had purchased from the Emperor of Byzantium for a price three times the construction costs of the church.

PLATE 37

Paris

Intérieur de la Ste-Chapelle, le Chœur

Here we see the shimmering beauty of the interior of Sainte-Chapelle. Even this stunning depiction fails to capture the beauty of this space, as the light passing through the colored stained glass that lines its walls cannot be depicted in black and white. The diversity of color appears to be regular here, as the decorative motifs seem to repeat again and again.

PLATE 38

Le Panthéon

The Panthéon, dedicated to the great men of the French nation—as the inscription on the building states—stands regally in the late-day sun. It seems to be a solemn occasion—still and quiet—fitting for the building in which these citizens' remains lie. It was built in the eighteenth century to be a church, but was completed just as the Revolution began and was quickly reimagined by Voltaire to serve its current function. During the tumultuous nineteenth century, it became a church again for short periods, but has since returned to serve the state. Just after this photograph was taken, Sadi Carnot, the French President, was interred in the Panthéon after having been assassinated by an anarchist.

PLATE 39

Paris

Le Luxembourg

Although this is meant to be a photograph of a monument—the Luxembourg Palace and its garden—it is more a family portrait, a rare image in this album. The family of eight strolls through the garden on a day off, dressed to the nines. It is a perfect representation of the rise of leisure time in the city, especially in the seventeenth-century gardens of the queen, Marie de Medici, here open to the public for personal pleasure.

PLATE 40

L'Avenue du Bois de Boulogne

The carriages and their passengers shown here are leaving Paris for greener pastures. The Neurdein Frères have captured another moment of leisure in the 1890s, the path well-trodden by Parisians leaving the city on the Avenue Foch from the Arc de Triomphe toward the vast Bois de Boulogne, an enormous stretch of woods, parks, and activities.

La Grand Lac

Although the Bois de Boulogne had existed since the Middle Ages as a hunting ground and as a site of royal residences, under Napoleon III it was reimagined as the largest public park in Paris, built to serve the changing tastes of the middle classes who wanted to spend their free time and the weekends away from the city. Depicted here is the man-made lower lake, with one of its islands in the center. We see that the lake was intended to be walked around—note the path on the left side—a predecessor of many urban parks today.

PLATE 42

La Cascade

The Grand Cascade, constructed in the 1850s to feed water from the Bois de Boulogne's upper lake to the lower lake (see Plate 42), is reminiscent of the Buttes-Chaumont (see Plate 34). Both works of impressive engineering, these dramatic natural landscapes were standard practice in late nineteenth-century French urban landscaping.

La Grande Cascade

This photograph of a different Grand Cascade is the only photo the Neurdein brothers chose to include from the historic Parc de Saint-Cloud, located south of the Bois de Boulogne just outside of Paris. The château on the park's grounds, which many important monarchs, aristocrats, and officials had called their residence since the sixteenth century, was left in ruins in 1870 during the Franco-Prussian War when the French army attacked the Prussians, who were using the site as a base. In this photograph, the two seventeenth-century fountains—the upper from the 1660s and the lower from thirty years later, designed by Hardouin-Mansart (see his Invalides in Plate 17)—remind us of the glory the château once had. While the fountains remain standing, the château's ruins were demolished in 1892.

PLATE 44

Façade Principale

This photograph of the entrance to the Versailles Palace is a surprising image for the Neurdein Frères. First, it is taken off-center from the entrance and therefore appears asymmetrical. The horizon is also not perfectly flat and the low position of the camera gives the imperfect ground prominence in the image, making the 700-room palace look small. It looks much more like a snapshot than a postcard image, all the more interesting considering that this is one of the great French monuments.

La Chambre de Louis XIV

Louis XIV's bedroom at the Versailles Palace is, like Plate 45, depicted in an unconventional manner for the Neurdein Frères. Unlike the other interiors in the album, the light is not soft and magical—there is glare off the bed and the paintings on the right side of the bed. As we see, the palace was already functioning as a museum, though the decoration of the rooms has since been reorganized. Louis, featured in a profile portrait to the left of his bed, looks on.

PLATE 46

La Galerie des Batailles

The Galerie des Batailles in the Versailles Palace was an early nineteenth-century creation under the reign of Louis Philippe, who wanted to appropriate unused apartments in the palace to create a grand hall. The paintings lining the walls were chosen to represent the great military battles in French history—from Clovis in the fifth century to Napoleon. This gallery was significantly damaged in the 1978 bombing of the palace by Breton nationalists.

PLATE 47

Le Bapin de Latone & le Tapis Vert

This picture captures a scene that could have come out of an Impressionist painting. With the camera perched high up behind the Château de Versailles, it looks out onto a scene of a pleasurable day in the gardens, with Parisians and tourists of all types relaxing and enjoying the museum and its grounds. While people's clothes have changed since the 1890s, their activities have not.

PLATE 48

Voiture du Sacre de Charles X

The most luxurious of all carriages was here on display at the museum in Versailles. Charles X's carriage from 1830, designed for his coronation, was covered in gold. It was considered to be made at such a high, almost unachievable, level of craftsmanship that it was used again by Napoleon III during his own coronation (note his "N" emblem on the fabric of the carriage).

La Maison du Seigneur

This rustic residence on the Versailles grounds, the Queen's Hamlet, was built by Marie An-toinette in the 1780s. Almost like a private Epcot Center of the time, it was intended to be a re-creation of a traditional Norman village around a lake and to give the queen a country retreat just minutes away from the palace.

PARIS IN PHOTOGRAPHS, 1890s

Printed and Bound in China by C & C Joint Printing CO., (GUANGDONG) LTD.
Composed in Kennerley, typeface designed by Andrew Leman in 2002.

Printed on 157 gsm matte art paper.

DISTRIBUTED BY DOVER PUBLICATIONS, INC.